Perspectives

Extinction Is Forever
Or Is It?

T0359546

Flying Start
to Literacy®

Contents

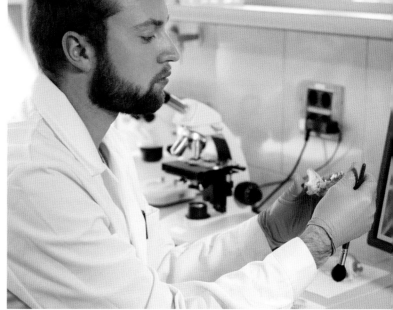

Introduction

Should we bring back extinct species?

When a species becomes extinct, not one of that plant or animal exists in the world. And in today's world, animal species are becoming extinct at a rapid rate. But now scientists think they have worked out a way to bring some of them back.

Many people have questions: Is it the right thing to do? Which animals should be brought back? Where would they live?

And some people think we should focus on saving endangered species, before *they* become extinct.

What do scientists need to think about before such decisions are made?

What have we lost???

To date, there have been five mass extinctions, during which huge numbers of plant and animal species were wiped out in a short period of time.

Now, we may be in a sixth mass extinction – this one caused by humans, writes Joshua Hatch.

What are we in danger of losing? How can we stop it?

Before humans became a dominant species on Earth, there were five so-called mass extinctions on the planet. These extinctions wiped out an astonishing number of plant and animal species.

The first extinction happened about 439 million years ago. An ice age and falling sea levels wiped out about 86 per cent of life on our planet.

The remaining plant and animal species that survived continued to live and evolve until the second mass extinction 80 million years later. This one appears to have been caused by widespread volcanic activity and killed about 75 per cent of Earth's species.

An illustration of the extinct marine animal called *Caryocrinites oratus* that existed over 400 million years ago

Then, about 252 million years ago, a supervolcano erupted and filled the atmosphere with carbon dioxide. The earth warmed and the oceans turned acidic. This mass extinction was particularly bad – 96 per cent of species on the planet perished.

For the next 50 million years, things seemed okay. About 200 million years ago, the earth's climate started to heat up and caused another mass extinction. This allowed the dinosaurs to take over the earth, which they did for about 130 million years.

Then, about 65 million years ago, huge volcanoes erupted and a giant asteroid struck the planet. This time, the dinosaurs weren't so lucky. They, and about three-quarters of life on Earth, were wiped out. This allowed mammals, including humans, to increase numbers.

439 million years ago	364 million years ago	252 million years ago
Ordovician-Silurian extinction	Late Devonian extinction	Permian-Triassic extinction

Today, every plant and animal species currently on Earth descends from organisms that survived these mass extinctions.

We may now be in a sixth mass extinction. This chart shows estimates for how many species have been lost in each of the past five centuries:

Years	Approximate number of species to go extinct
1500–1600	54
1600–1700	22
1700–1800	60
1800–1900	144
1900–2000	500

Over the past 300 years, people have been responsible for the extinction of a growing number of plant and animal species. What are we in danger of losing?

214 to 199 million years ago	65 million years ago	Present
Triassic-Jurassic extinction	Cretaceous-Paleogene extinction	Holocene epoch

Bring back the mammoth:

An expert's view

Beth Shapiro is an expert scientist who helped unlock the process of de-extinction – bringing back an extinct species. In this interview, science writer Joseph Taylor asks Beth about some of the tricky issues surrounding de-extinction.

After reading this interview with Beth, think about your opinion. What do you think about de-extinction?

During the last ice age, animals that looked like large hairy elephants roamed Asia and the Americas. But by about 4,000 years ago, all the mammoths and mastodons had vanished. Some scientists are saying that one day we might be able to bring these ancient beasts back to life. And what about other extinct animals? Maybe we could bring them back, too? Let's see what expert scientist Beth Shapiro thinks.

Joseph: Is de-extinction possible? What are the issues we must overcome?

Beth: Whether it's the mammoth or the passenger pigeon or the dodo or some other extinct species, there's a different suite of technical, ethical and ecological challenges that would be associated with bringing them back to life. Some of these challenges are not solved, and some of them are really hard to solve – it varies by species.

Issues to think about...

Technical	Ethical	Ecological
HOW do we do it? Is everything we need available? And if it is, what needs to be done with the animals?	SHOULD we do it? Is it the right thing to do? And who makes this decision?	WHERE would the animal live? What would it eat? What impact would the animal's return have on an ecosystem?

Joseph: What if scientists overcame all the technical issues involved in bringing back a mammoth, and they were able to do it? Should they do it? Is it the right thing to do?

Beth: I think that if the goal is to bring back a mammoth so you could say, "I brought back a mammoth and put it in a zoo so we can stare at it and say, 'Oh, look. There's a mammoth.' . . . " then I'm not sure that's the ethical thing to do. If we're going to go through the trouble of resurrecting things, then we should really have ironed out why we're going to do it.

Joseph: So let's say then that we bring back the mammoth and we don't put it in a zoo. Instead, we let it live in the wild – would that work?

Beth: Well, I think that a key goal of de-extinction should be restoring once-thriving ecosystems so that the animals have their natural habitat to begin living in. So if a mammoth was created, we would need to think about where it would live and what it would eat. One other question is – do we know why the animal went extinct? And if we do, have we solved the problem that caused it to go extinct in the first place?

Key steps to bring back a mammoth

Scientists know what needs to be done to bring a mammoth back from extinction, but they don't know if it would work. Here's what would have to happen.

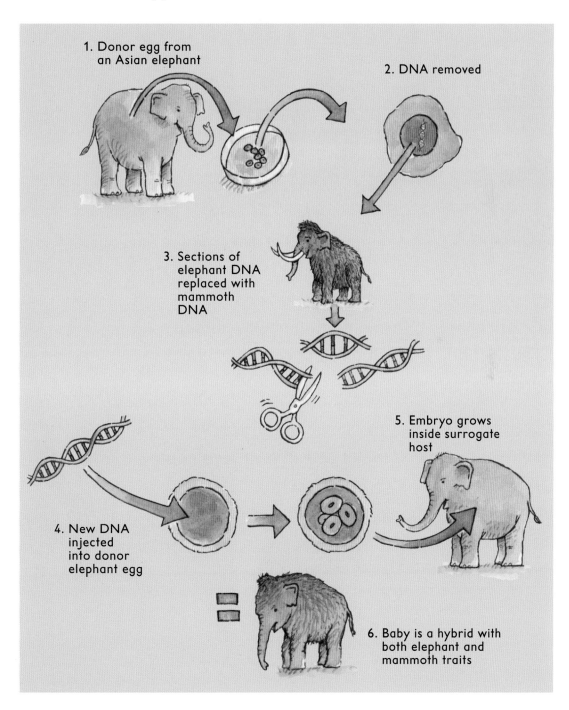

1. Donor egg from an Asian elephant

2. DNA removed

3. Sections of elephant DNA replaced with mammoth DNA

4. New DNA injected into donor elephant egg

5. Embryo grows inside surrogate host

6. Baby is a hybrid with both elephant and mammoth traits

The Tasmanian tiger

In Australia, the Tasmanian tiger was hunted to extinction. It is gone forever – or is it? asks Kerrie Shanahan.

Scientists now have the technology to reverse its extinction. Does it make sense to devote money, expertise and time to bring back this fascinating animal? Why should they do it – or not?

The Tasmanian tiger (*Thylacinus cynocephalus*) was a carnivorous marsupial that lived in the bush throughout Tasmania. There were about 5,000 of these unique animals left before the government placed a bounty on them – it paid people to hunt and kill them. By 1936, there were no Tasmanian tigers left. They were extinct.

Associate Professor Andrew Pask is a scientist, and he believes we must bring back the Tasmanian tiger:

"We have a social responsibility, we exterminated the Tasmanian tiger . . . I think it is a very real discussion then to bring these animals back and reintroduce them to the environment."

Andrew explains why
the Tasmanian tiger is a
particularly good fit to be the first
animal brought back from extinction:

> *"The Tasmanian wilderness is very similar to how it was in 1936 when the last animal went extinct. The animals that it ate are still there, it could move back into that food chain and that ecological niche."*

Other scientists and ecologists agree with Andrew. They believe that because the Tasmanian tiger recently became extinct, bringing it back will not disrupt the ecosystem. Instead, it could play a really important and critical role. What do you think?

Could *Jurassic Park* really happen?

In the movie *Jurassic Park*, scientists used dinosaur DNA to bring extinct dinosaurs back to life. In real life, scientists don't have access to dinosaur DNA and probably never will. But if they did, could they bring dinosaurs back? Could a version of *Jurassic Park* really take place?

Here's how some students answered this question. Which perspective do you agree with? What is your view?

I think that it truly could happen. We could find a mosquito that was preserved, and we have the knowledge to extract blood from it, and this blood could have dinosaur DNA in it. From there, anything is possible!

Jurassic Park could become true. I think that scientists could find fossilised dinosaur eggs. They could then bring them to a lab and hatch them. The scientists could provide food for them and somewhere for them to live . . . as long as the dinosaurs don't end up eating the scientists!

I believe that dinosaurs on Earth in the 21st or 22nd century are a possibility. It is completely feasible. But I believe firmly that messing around with nature is a big mistake. The dinosaurs became extinct because they weren't meant to survive. Bringing them back could change life and the way we live it, forever.

DNA tests might give scientists knowledge about dinosaurs, but I find it absurd for anyone to think that a million-year-old drop of deoxyribonucleic acid [DNA] could bring back an ancient extinct reptile.

"If it's gone, it's gone!"

One extinct species that gets a lot of attention is the woolly mammoth because scientists have discovered frozen samples of its DNA – the ingredient that makes de-extinction possible.

But restoring the woolly mammoth to its natural environment would cost a lot of money, argues Joshua Hatch. Would this money be better spent on saving animals that are currently endangered and at risk of becoming extinct? Are you convinced by his arguments? If so, why?

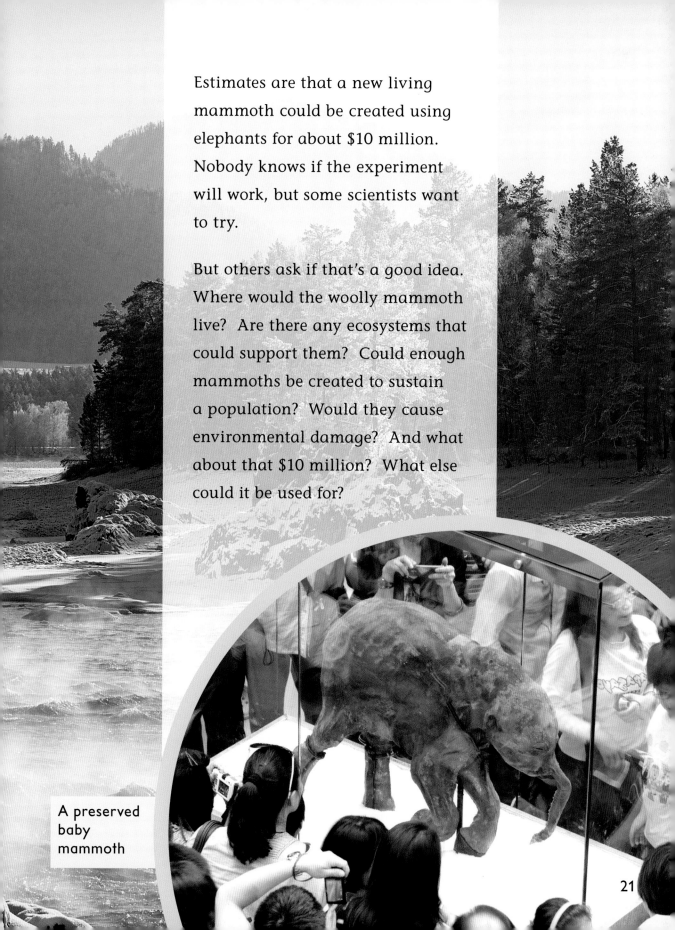

Estimates are that a new living mammoth could be created using elephants for about $10 million. Nobody knows if the experiment will work, but some scientists want to try.

But others ask if that's a good idea. Where would the woolly mammoth live? Are there any ecosystems that could support them? Could enough mammoths be created to sustain a population? Would they cause environmental damage? And what about that $10 million? What else could it be used for?

A preserved baby mammoth

Many conservationists say we should concentrate on saving the animals and plants that are endangered today, instead of trying to bring back those that have been lost. "If it's gone, it's gone!" they argue. "So let's not let other species die out." At this time, there are more than 16,000 species that are considered endangered.

It's a lot cheaper to save existing species than to resurrect extinct ones. Conservationists say we could save tigers for about $10,000 per cat. Instead of spending $10 million to bring back one mammoth, we could save a thousand tigers.

Isn't that a smarter use of the money? Plus, by saving tigers, we would help preserve ecosystems that are home to other endangered species, too.

Another argument against resurrecting extinct species is that people will worry less about protecting the ones we still have. You don't want people thinking: *We can always bring them back later.*

De-extinction, as it's called, is not a solution. It's an idea and one we should not resort to. So let's save the animals and plants we have now. It's cheaper, easier, more effective – and the right thing to do. Save de-extinction for science fiction.

What is your opinion? How to write a persuasive argument

1. State your opinion

Think about the issues related to your topic. What is your opinion?

2. Research

Research the information you need to support your opinion.

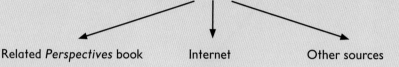

Related *Perspectives* book   Internet   Other sources

3. Make a plan

Introduction

How will you "hook" the reader?

State your opinion.

List reasons to support your opinion.

What persuasive devices will you use?

Reason 1
Support your reason with evidence and details.

Reason 2
Support your reason with evidence and details.

Reason 3
Support your reason with evidence and details.

Conclusion

Restate your opinion. Leave your reader with a strong message.

4. Publish

Publish your persuasive argument.

Use visuals to reinforce your opinion.